Portchester C

John Goodall

Introduction

Portchester Castle is set within the magnificently preserved walls of a Roman fort, the most complete example north of the Alps. It stands imposingly on a low-lying tongue of land that projects into the natural harbour of Portsmouth. The Roman fort was probably established here in the AD 280s. From the fifth century, a Saxon community settled this fort, and in about 904 it was turned into a stronghold, or burgh, one in a chain intended to protect the kingdom of Wessex from Viking raids.

Following the Norman Conquest in 1066, the Roman fort walls became the defensive perimeter of a great castle. Its principal buildings were set in an enclosure in the north-west angle of the Roman defences. Diagonally opposite, in the outer bailey, stands the parish church — all that remains of a monastic foundation established here in about 1128. Among the castle buildings that survive today are the 12th-century great tower, or keep, and a royal residence erected in the 1390s for Richard II.

Portchester remained important for successive English kings because of its position by a harbour, with easy access to the Continent. The castle remained occupied into the 17th century. It then served intermittently as a prisoner-of-war camp until the end of the Napoleonic wars. The last prisoners left Portchester Castle by May 1814, and it was finally abandoned by the Army in 1819. The castle was taken into state guardianship in the early 20th century and extensively repaired with cheap labour during the Depression.

Above: The tomb of Sir Thomas Cornwallis in the church of St Mary. Cornwallis was constable of the castle in the early 17th century

Facing page: View of the Watergate and church of St Mary, seen from across the harbour

3

Tour

Since they were constructed over 1,700 years ago, the walls, towers and enclosing ditches of the square-planned Roman fort at Portchester have been the constant and defining element of this site. Within the huge nine-acre area they enclose, great changes have taken place. As it exists today, the layout broadly reflects the medieval arrangement of the site, with a great tower, or keep, at one corner, surrounded by other important castle buildings in the inner bailey.

FOLLOWING THE TOUR

The tour begins in the inner bailey of the medieval castle. Visitors are then taken round the outside of the Roman fortifications and back through the Watergate to the church of St Mary.

The small numbered plans in the margins highlight key points on the tour.

▮ INNER BAILEY

The inner bailey was the medieval heart of Portchester Castle. Around this square-planned courtyard, dominated by the massive form of the 12th-century keep, are the shells of several grand medieval ranges. The inner bailey was probably laid out when the castle was first established in the late 11th century. It sits in the north-west corner of the Roman fort and is divided from the remainder of the fort enclosure by an L-shaped ditch and wall. All the original buildings and fortifications of the inner bailey at Portchester are likely to have been of earth and timber. But in the early 12th century these began to be replaced in stone. One of the first new stone buildings was the keep, which was probably begun in about 1130.

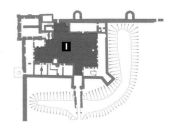

Below: A view of the inner bailey and keep, with the ruined forebuilding beneath

Facing page: Spiral staircase in the keep

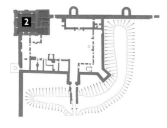

Below: *A view of the keep from outside the castle walls. The small, square sockets in the walls were used to support scaffolding*

☑ KEEP AND FOREBUILDING

This tower has always been the architectural showpiece and symbolic focus of the castle. Built on a square plan, it stands more than 30m (100ft) high, and its thick walls are faced with small, beautifully cut stones. In the 12th century, the keep contained some of the most important apartments in the castle. Despite its uniform appearance today, the keep was built in three stages. As it was first completed in the 1130s, it rose to a point approximately level with the tops of the buttresses around the exterior. But probably within 20 years of its completion, this low structure was greatly increased in height with the addition of two upper storeys. Finally the crown

of the building was raised in the 1320s. During the 1390s the basement of the tower was vaulted, and several new windows were inserted in the principal first-floor chambers.

As is typical of 12th-century keeps, that at Portchester has its main entrance at first-floor level. This was approached up an external stair housed within a subsidiary tower, or forebuilding. The forebuilding was altered extensively over the Middle Ages and is now largely ruined. The modern wooden stair, built up against the bailey wall, follows the line of a lost 12th-century predecessor. At ground level, immediately to the left of the stair, was a prison chamber and above this a chapel. The blind arch in the wall of the keep would originally have faced into the chapel interior and might have served as an architectural frame for the king's throne when he attended services here. Above the arch are the incised lines of different roofs, evidence of the many alterations the forebuilding has undergone.

To the right of the wooden stair, within a tower projecting beyond the Roman wall, was a large, first-floor chamber. It possibly served as a waiting room for visitors to the keep and was provided in the later Middle Ages with a grand bay window, probably inserted about 1489; the remains of a contemporary window on the south courtyard face of the forebuilding are decorated with a shield bearing the arms of Henry VII (reigned 1485–1509). Archaeological excavation of the inner bailey has revealed that in the 1320s the forebuilding was surrounded by other buildings, and a new main stair to the keep was erected. No trace of these buildings now remains above ground, but a diagonal line of sockets – the settings for the steps of the 1320s stair – is visible in the east face of the forebuilding.

First Floor

Our understanding of the keep as a living medieval building is complicated by the many alterations it has undergone, in particular the insertion of extra floors to lodge 3,000 prisoners during the Napoleonic wars. It is arranged today on four levels, separated by three modern timber floors, and is divided through almost its full height by a central or spine wall, creating two principal chambers on each floor. Access between the floors was originally provided only by a spiral stair in the south-west angle of the building, but a modern wooden stair now also rises up the northern side of the keep from the first floor.

The first-floor chambers of the keep were probably intended to function together in the 12th century as a suite of rooms. Although now badly damaged and comfortless, the room entered directly from the forebuilding stair is likely to have been used for receiving important visitors. To the left of the entrance, in the south-east corner of the chamber, is a well and in the adjacent south wall are two large and richly

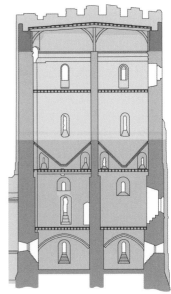

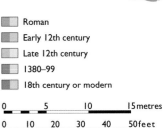

	Roman
	Early 12th century
	Late 12th century
	1380–99
	18th century or modern

0   5   10   15 metres
0 10 20 30 40 50 feet

Above: A cross-section of the keep looking westwards. The building is divided by a central spine wall and was raised in three main stages. The V-shaped outlines of the original roof are visible within what is now the second floor of the building

Above: The top floor of the keep.
The roof is modern, and sits within
the crown of the building

Below: It is still possible to see
the line of the original roof inside
the second-floor level of the keep

1 Original V-shaped line of roof

2 Beams used as racking for
prisoners' hammocks during
the Napoleonic wars

ornamented windows, one of which is now blocked. There is
also a latrine in the thickness of the outer wall at the far end
of the room, though access to this is now obstructed by
concrete beams inserted to stabilize the keep in the 1930s.
The room originally had a flat, panelled wooden ceiling, some
fixings for which still remain. Richly painted and furnished this
would have been a splendid interior in the 12th century.

The second chamber is entered through the doorway at
the far (west) end of the central partition wall. This must have
served as an inner apartment, possibly a bedroom or
withdrawing chamber. Although entirely devoid of architectural
ornament, it is the only room in the keep with a fireplace, now
a ragged opening in the centre of the outside wall to your
left. There was no proper chimney, and the smoke escaped
through openings in the wall. In the north-east corner of the
chamber is a small latrine. The door of this has been ripped
away, but a little wall niche for a candle is still visible.

Second Floor

Before the keep was first heightened in the mid-12th century,
the roof of the building was set within this second-floor level.
Indeed, projecting from the end walls of both chambers is a
narrow ledge of stone that clearly follows the V-shaped
outline of a double-pitched roof. In its original form, therefore,
this floor must have consisted of a series of loft spaces, lit at
either end by small windows. Directly accessible from the
main spiral stair, these lofts might have been used for storage,
or to lodge members of the household or servants.

When the keep was raised in about 1150, this roof level became a floor. But the fact that the redundant lines of the original keep roof are preserved here indicates that no attempt was made to finish off the interiors of this new floor as comfortable apartments. Rather, it seems as if the keep was heightened simply to turn it into a much taller building; the second floor was raised to a height of nearly 10m (30ft) and a top storey was added. This upper level had a latrine chamber and was clearly intended for domestic use. But, as its plain architectural detailing suggests, the comforts of the top storey can never have approached those of the first-floor apartments, and it possibly served as a guardchamber.

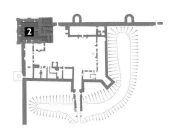

The massive internal spaces of the upper section of the keep have been variously partitioned since the Middle Ages. Judging from the socket marks that cover the walls, numerous timbers have been removed from within it. Some of these relate to lost floors inserted between the medieval levels, but others served as racking on which prisoners of war slung their hammocks during the Napoleonic wars.

Third Floor and Roof

When the keep was first heightened in about 1150, the roof was replaced at the level where the central partition wall terminates. Another floor was added, perhaps around 1320, and the roof raised to its present position. The inserted floor has now been removed and the roof is modern.

Below: A view of the castle, harbour and parish church of St Mary from the keep roof

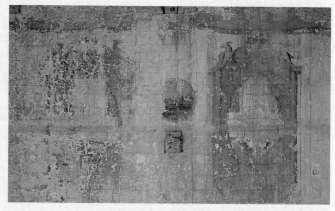

The Castle Theatre

Along the side walls is a series of landscape scenes, one of which depicts Portchester Castle

Faintly visible on the walls on the second floor of the keep are the remains of an elaborate painted decorative scheme for the auditorium of an early 19th-century theatre. The scheme attempts to create the illusion of an interior hung with rich objects: along the side walls is a series of panels within elaborate frames, and between them are small landscape scenes, one of which depicts Portchester Castle. Swags of fabric are painted around the tops of the walls. Very little is known about the history of this theatre. In the Napoleonic period, when the castle housed prisoners of war, we know that plays were put on here, and it is possible that the theatre was established in this period. However, the painted decoration must date from after 1830, despite its Continental style, as it includes French Ultramarine, a pigment that only came into use after this date. A local historian, J H Cooke, writing in 1930, said that a Mr Sutton had put on plays in the keep. So far, this vague reference is the nearest thing we have to an explanation for this mysterious decorative scheme.

Above: The remains of an elaborate decorative scheme on the walls of the theatre in the keep, including a picture of the castle, shown as a detail on the left

Below: A reconstruction drawing of the theatre, completed after 1830

❸ RICHARD II'S PALACE

Extending from the foot of the keep around the west and
south sides of the inner bailey are the remains of a grand
series of residential apartments built by Richard II (r.1377–99)
as part of his reorganization of the castle between 1396 and
1399. There are two principal ranges, both two storeys high.
The one to the south is the public and service wing, which
contained the great hall and kitchens. To the west are the
royal apartments, including the king's great chamber.

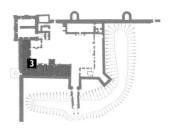

    The principal chambers in each range are on the first
floor, marked out on the exterior of the building by the tall
windows. These upper chambers were connected by a vaulted
passage at the angle of the courtyard, and a medieval visitor
would have moved through them in a particular sequence,
from the public great hall to the king's innermost chamber.
Such planning is typical of palace interiors of this period.

    Beneath this suite of royal apartments were several
rooms, each accessible through a separate door from the
courtyard. These have smaller windows than the rooms
on the floor above and were probably used for storage
and accommodation.

Porch

Entrance to the royal apartments on the first floor was
through the projecting porch in the middle of the great hall
range. To either side of its entrance are two curious pedestals
with hat-shaped covers set above them. These are housings
for lamps to light the threshold. Rising up from this entrance
door was a stair, now lost, to the first-floor door of the hall.

*Above: The door of the great hall
porch, with brackets for
lamps to light the threshold*
*Below: A French manuscript
illustration of Richard II, who built
a series of grand apartments at
Portchester in the late 14th century*

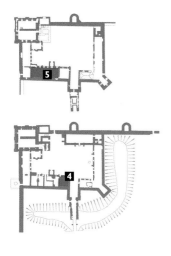

This stair was covered by a miniature stone vault, of which the stubs remain. Above the vault was a tiny chamber, reached by a spiral stair from the porch landing.

4 Kitchen

The great hall range is now a roofless shell, incorporating the 12th-century inner bailey wall along its south side. It is divided into two unequal areas by a stone wall. The smaller of these is the kitchen. Partitioning the kitchen from the rest of the range was probably intended as a safeguard against the spread of fire. The kitchen is very small by medieval standards and was presumably served by a centrally placed fire. A building account records that in 1398 a louvre was erected to release the smoke. Food would have been carried into the great hall via a stair (now ruined) through the raised door in one corner of the kitchen.

5 Great Hall

To the west of the kitchen wall, the range was divided into an upper and lower level by a wooden floor. Stone walls separated the ground-floor chambers, and the lines of these are still visible.

In the small area between the kitchen wall and the porch door, an intermediate floor was inserted to create three rectangular chambers on ground-, first- and second-floor levels. The uppermost chamber, which also had access to the room over the porch, might have been the lodging of a senior household servant. But the two chambers beneath are likely

Below: A view of the exterior of the great hall range. To the left of the porch are the service rooms. Beyond the porch is the great hall and to the far right is the great chamber range. (For key, see reconstruction drawing on opposite page)

A RECONSTRUCTION DRAWING OF THE INNER BAILEY AFTER IT WAS REMODELLED IN THE 1390s

Richard II may never have seen his new palace, but this drawing shows how it might have been prepared for a royal visit, with furniture, hangings and tapestries. All the principal chambers are clearly identifiable. The first-floor rooms of the keep and the south-west chamber were probably withdrawing chambers, and the forebuilding stair would have offered private access to them. The exchequer chamber was presumably for royal business.

1 Kitchen

2 Buttery and pantry

3 Great hall

4 South-west chamber

5 Great chamber

6 Exchequer chamber

7 Chapel

8 First-floor rooms of the keep

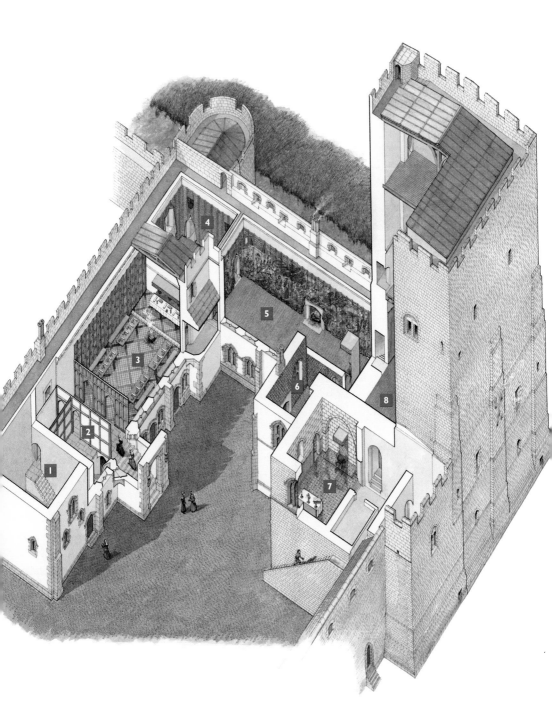

Above: A late 15th-century illustration of Richard II dining with the dukes of York, Gloucester and Ireland, just as he might have done at Portchester
Below: Within the north wall of the great hall are these fragments of richly carved arches, the remains of 12th-century buildings

to have been service chambers – probably a buttery and pantry – and were connected internally by a flight of steps, the base for which survives.

The remainder of the upper floor was occupied by the great hall. This must have been a splendid chamber, open to the roof and lit down one side by high windows. According to the building accounts, the glass in the windows of this and the other principal chambers was decorated with coats of arms and heraldic borders. The hall was heated by a fire set centrally on an open hearth, the square foundation for which remains at ground level. Along the top of the windowless south wall are fragments of a carved stone frieze that originally ran round the interior. Like the wall frieze of the great hall at Westminster, London, perhaps Richard II's most celebrated building, it appears to depict heraldic beasts. The blank wall might also have been decorated with wall-paintings; during royal visits it was doubtless intended to be hung with tapestries, of which Richard II had a large collection.

A medieval visitor would not have entered directly into the hall from the porch. As was typical in English great halls, the main entrance as well as the kitchen and service doors were concealed from the body of the room by a screen. The area enclosed by this partition was known as the screen's passage. It was located at what was termed the 'low' end of

the hall, the area commonly accessible to the whole household and its servants. At the opposite end was the 'high' end of the hall, where the king's table stood, raised on a dais. The building accounts suggest that a timber canopy was set up over the table to indicate its importance. Other tables would have lined the sides of the room between the dais and the screen's passage, and members of the household would have sat at these in strict hierarchical order.

To be allowed to pass beyond the great hall into the chamber range was a mark of distinction. To do so, a visitor would have had to walk up onto the dais and through the door in the north wall to the right. From here a vaulted passage leads to the upper floor of the adjacent range, where the king's inner apartments were located. Immediately below the dais doorway in the north wall of the great hall range are the remains of two richly carved arches. From their detailing these would appear to date from the early 12th century and show that Richard II's ranges incorporate the remains of much earlier buildings. The 14th-century arrangements of the great hall range compare closely to the abbot of Westminster's house, which was built in the 1370s and still survives at Westminster. Both buildings were designed by royal masons.

Left: The great hall at Portchester
Below: Fragments of glass, which may once have formed part of the great hall windows

Above: A reconstruction drawing of the castle in the early 17th century, following the alterations made by Sir Thomas Cornwallis to the east range. In 1609 the new range was described as 'containing four fair lodging chambers above and as many rooms for office below'

6 Great Chamber Range and the Exchequer Chamber

The passage from the dais of the great hall led into the larger of two rooms that occupied the upper floor of the west or great chamber range. This was probably the king's great chamber, or formal reception room, and was heated by a large, central fireplace, now a ragged hole in the wall. To the south of the great chamber, and divided from it by a stone wall, was a small room, which might have been the royal bedchamber. Both this room and that immediately below it have windows arranged like fireplaces, with narrow flues letting in light from small holes (now blocked) in the wall above. Presumably this was a defensive measure, reflecting the builders' reluctance to insert large windows in the inner bailey wall. Running beneath the great chamber were two rooms, each with a brick-backed fireplace.

The outline of the lost, low-pitched roof to the great chamber range is still etched on the keep wall. Beneath this, the line of another single-pitch roof from an earlier range is also visible. Opening off the great chamber range beneath the keep are two further rooms built by Richard II. Their original function is not known, but the upper room might have been the 'exchequer chamber', a room for financial and legal work, described in the 1390s building accounts. A door from this chamber connects with the forebuilding chapel and the keep beyond.

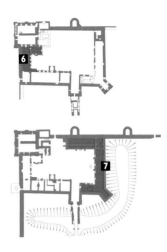

7 EAST RANGES

Little now remains of the three ranges that enclosed the east end of the inner bailey. To the north are the foundations of a 12th-century building that served in the late Middle Ages as the residence of the constable of the castle. It comprised a hall and vaulted undercroft and was remodelled several times. Ashton's Tower, at the east end of the residence, was begun by a constable of that name who served here between 1376 and 1381. A building account records that the tower was completed in 1385, also that work to the 'knight's chamber' – possibly the chamber over the Roman bastion behind the constable's hall – was then underway. The chambers within Ashton's Tower served as an extension to the constable's residence.

Extending across the bailey to the south of Ashton's Tower is a ruined stone range. In the 13th century this was only one storey high, and housed a storeroom or stable to the north and a kitchen to the south. By the end of the 14th century the range had been largely rebuilt, one end of it being absorbed into the constable's residence. This structure was completely remodelled in the early 17th century by the last constable of the castle, Sir Thomas Cornwallis. These alterations were part of a wider project to remodel the whole of the constable's house.

The south range now houses the ticket office and shop. It was also remodelled by Cornwallis as a kitchen, and the walls incorporate many reused fragments of Romanesque sculpture.

Left: A view of the east range, looking towards Ashton's Tower, completed in 1385, as an extension to the constable's residence

Above: The Landgate viewed from across the inner bailey moat

Below: View of the inner moat and gatehouse with the angle tower to the right

Facing page: The medieval north postern gate is in the same place as its Roman predecessor

◪ INNER BAILEY MOAT AND GATEHOUSE

The wall that encloses the inner bailey is faced with small blocks of cut stone, an early 12th-century style of masonry similar to that of the keep. Originally, it would have had a battlemented parapet running along the top of it. At the angle of the moat is a fine, projecting 12th-century tower built on a square plan with an open back.

In the Middle Ages, the moat around the bailey was probably deeper and wider than it is today. Its inner bank would also have been higher, concealing the clearly defined band of rubble masonry along the foot of the wall. This detail is clearest in the east wall of the bailey. The moat originally extended round the entire circuit of the inner bailey, both within and outside the Roman fort enclosure. Fed from the sea, a culvert below ground level allowed water to pass between its inner and outer sections. The medieval moat had largely silted up by the 18th century, when the eastern stretch was re-cut as a swimming-pool for prisoners. It was re-created in its present form some time after 1926.

An open-backed tower projecting from the bailey wall formed the original gatehouse between the medieval inner bailey and the surrounding Roman fort enclosure. This tower

still survives but its fortifications were subsequently extended forward in stages. Immediately in front of it stands a vaulted porch of the 1320s, closed by a portcullis. This is flanked on either side by the remains of small, D-shaped towers (see the plan on the inside back cover). Built beyond these is a long, walled passage with a drawbridge pit beneath, probably of the 1380s. At the end of this passage are two square towers, built in about 1600 to operate a second drawbridge over the moat.

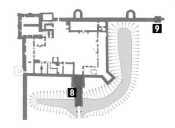

9 OUTER BAILEY
North Postern Gate
This postern, or side gate, stands in the position of a Roman predecessor, also a small arched opening in the wall. It was one of the four original entrances into the fort enclosure. The inner face of the Roman wall, to the left of the gate, has been roughly hacked away – the result of medieval quarrying to provide building stone for the castle. Only around the inner bailey is the Roman wall of its original thickness. The D-shaped bastions or towers, which are an integral part of the Roman walls, were originally hollow. Though some remain so, notably those flanking the Watergate by the church, many were filled in and walled up during the medieval period.

Above: Aerial view of Portchester, showing the outline of the Roman walls

Below: A reconstruction of the Landgate as it might have appeared in Roman times, standing behind the line of the wall

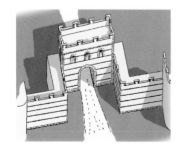

⑩ NORTH WALL

The medieval defences have been seemlessly incorporated into the Roman wall, with its towers. Its exterior is of particular interest because it features a mid-14th-century cannon fortification, one of the earliest-known examples in English architecture. Running along the wall head is a covered passage with gun loops, many now badly damaged. This gallery runs unbroken around the inside of Ashton's Tower. From the tower a door in the gallery opens onto the wall-walk of the outer bailey. Beyond Ashton's Tower is one of the Roman D-shaped towers. Bridging the angle between it and the wall is a large arch, an outlet for a series of medieval latrines.

The keep stands across the north-west angle of the Roman fort, which must have been demolished to accommodate it. Projecting from the wall beneath it is the forebuilding, with the remains of an elaborate, 15th-century bay window. These two external façades of the keep are much plainer than those facing onto the inner bailey.

The ground-floor windows on the exterior of the keep are double-splayed – in other words, the opening is narrowest in the middle of the wall, not on its inner or outer face.

This rare arrangement has been cited as evidence that the keep encases an earlier building, which had slightly narrower windows. The date and precise form of such a structure, if it ever existed, remain a matter for speculation.

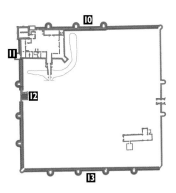

11 WEST WALL AND LOST TOWER

The Roman fort was laid out symmetrically. Around its square perimeter were 20 regularly spaced D-shaped towers, of which, remarkably, 16 remain. The square stone platform, projecting into the grass, is the foundation of one of the four lost towers; it was adapted to house latrines in the Middle Ages and demolished after 1790. It is possible to see how the foundations of the Roman fort were laid. The base of a trench about 1.5m (5ft) deep was filled with a mixture of flint and chalk and sealed with a layer of mortar. Laid into the mortar was a frame of squared timbers. It is the impression of these, long rotted away, that forms the channels in this foundation.

Above this, the D-shaped upper section of the tower, originally hollow and open-backed, was erected. Each tower had a drain to allow rainwater to escape from the interior. There is no evidence that any of the towers at Portchester projected above the level of the wall-walk or had any internal floors, unlike other Roman forts on the Continent. The raised doors in the wall here belong to the medieval reworking of this structure as a latrine tower.

12 LANDGATE

Set midway along each wall of the Roman fort was a gate: two principal ones to the east and west, and two secondary postern gates to the north and south (see page 19). The Landgate is a medieval reworking of the northern entrance to the fort. In its present form the gate dates largely from the 1390s and takes the form of a square tower with a vaulted gate passage and an upper lodging chamber. This chamber was later used as a detention cell for troublesome prisoners.

This building replaces an unusual Roman entrance arrangement, comparable to that found in the Roman fort of Pevensey in Sussex, down the coast. The Roman gatehouse was also rectangular in plan, with a central gate passage set between two ground-floor guard chambers. But it stood well behind the line of the wall, which turned inwards to meet it. Traces of a timber building erected within the Roman gate forecourt in the Anglo-Saxon period have been discovered.

13 SOUTH WALL

The south wall retains five of its original six towers. It is uninterrupted by additional medieval walls or gates, and gives the best impression of the original appearance of the Roman fort, though the battlements along the top of the wall are medieval. The original construction technique, with flint

Below: The Landgate, which stands within the forecourt of the original Roman fort enclosure. The inner arch of this largely 14th-century gate is Romanesque

interspersed with levelling courses of flat limestone slabs, or double courses of brick, are very clear, and the herringbone pattern of some of the flintwork can be seen. There is plenty of evidence for repair and patching in the walls, including the use of 19th-century brick to replicate the Roman tile courses. Towards the south-east corner of the fort, a row of nine square apertures in the wall are the outlets from the latrines of the 12th-century Augustinian monastery. The latrine structures within the fort walls have long since disappeared.

Looking across to Portsmouth harbour, under the Spinnaker tower, the masts of HMS *Victory* can be made out, and further to the right is the harbour entrance. Portchester was the first fortification to guard this magnificent natural harbour, beginning a development that includes the dockyard defences, and the mid-19th-century fortifications visible on the crest of Portsdown Hill to the north.

4 WATERGATE

The Watergate is a two-storey tower on a rectangular plan, originally with a lodging chamber on the upper floor. It stands on the main east–west axis of the fort and replaces a Roman entrance, identical to the one at the Landgate. With the exception of its innermost arch, the Watergate was largely built between 1321 and 1325. The innermost arch, with different coloured stones laid alternately, has been compared to that in the Anglo-Saxon church porch at nearby Titchfield and dated to the tenth century. But it may equally be an early Norman structure of the following century. The gate was subsequently damaged by the encroaching sea, as was the

Above: View of the 11th-century innermost arch of the Watergate
Below: The Watergate and Roman walls, seen from across the harbour

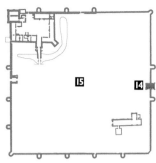

Roman wall along this side of the fort. Repairs to the gatehouse in 1369 probably included the construction of its front section, which projects beyond the line of the Roman wall. This addition was closed by a portcullis, the groove for which survives.

15 INTERIOR OF THE FORT

Little is known about the interior of the fort in the Roman period. It may never have been completed in the third century, and any remains have been largely destroyed by ploughing and later occupation. Most of the buildings in it were probably wooden and regularly laid out around the roads connecting the four entrances to the fort. The main road ran roughly along the line of the modern road between the Landgate and Watergate. It was lightly metalled and had a central drain.

Several Saxon buildings have been excavated on the site, but today nothing is visible of this period of occupation, with the possible exception of the arch of the Watergate. To the left stands the parish church of St Mary [not in the care of English Heritage]. The church is the only surviving building of a short-lived Augustinian monastery within the fort. It was founded in about 1128 but by 1150 had moved to a site at nearby Southwick, possibly because the castle lacked enough space. Judging from its architectural decoration, the church was probably under construction in the 1130s, though it is not known whether the structure or the monastic buildings were ever completed before the community moved.

The church is a rare, surviving example of the kind of building created to serve a modest, 12th-century monastery. Its font, located in the north-west corner of the nave, is a fine Romanesque example. In the churchyard are a number of interesting graves, notably those of W L Wyllie RA, the great maritime painter, and the recently restored grave of Thomas Goble RN. Goble was a master mariner on HMS *Victory* at the battle of Trafalgar, and following the death in action of the admiral's and captain's secretaries, acted as the last secretary to the fleet and to vice-admiral Lord Nelson.

Above: The church of St Mary, which was once part of the Augustinian monastery within the castle grounds
Below: W L Wyllie RA (1851–1931), the maritime painter, who is buried in the churchyard at Portchester

History

The commanding
position of Portchester
Castle, overlooking
Portsmouth harbour,
has ensured its vital role
in defending this stretch
of water. The Romans,
the Saxons and the
Normans all made use
of the natural defences
to protect themselves
from pirates and
raiders. The castle later
became an impressive
royal residence, and the
ideal departure point
for armies setting off for
the Continent. In later
years, the castle was
converted into a prison.

Left: Richard II (r.1377–99),
who remodelled Portchester Castle
extensively in the 1390s

ROMAN PORTCHESTER

It is not clear exactly when the Roman fort at Portchester was first established. But coin finds from recent excavations suggest that it was built by a certain Marcus Aurelius Carausius between AD 285 and 290. If this is correct, it allows us to determine in some detail the circumstances in which the fort was constructed.

Carausius rose to prominence during the reign of Emperor Diocletian and in 285 was commissioned to clear the North Sea of barbarian pirates. He was successful in his campaigns but was accused of enriching himself unscrupulously on the spoils of the pirates, only attacking their ships when they were laden with plunder. It is impossible to tell if this was true, but either for this reason or because of political jealousy, a plot was hatched to have Carausius executed. He heard of it and in response proclaimed himself emperor. Initially he controlled parts of Gaul (France) and Britain, but in 293 the last of his Continental possessions, Boulogne, was lost to the forces of Rome. Later that year he was assassinated by a follower called Alectus, who in turn proclaimed himself ruler of Britain. But in 296 a full-scale invasion of Britain finally brought the province back under central Roman authority.

The early development of Portchester Castle can be tied in very neatly with these events. Barbarian attacks along the coasts of Gaul and Britain were evidently a problem for the

Top: A coin minted by Carausius (d.293), self-proclaimed emperor and the builder of Portchester Castle
Above: A Roman leather shoe, found at Portchester
Below: A reconstruction drawing of the Roman fort at Portchester under construction between 285 and 290

Roman empire throughout the late third century, and to combat them, numerous forts were constructed or remodelled on both sides of the Channel. These have many features in common, in particular projecting D-shaped towers – a novel feature of Roman military architecture at this date. The forts probably acted as naval bases from which ships could intercept attacks by pirates as they sailed through the narrowing of the Channel towards the Straits of Dover. Commanding this natural bottleneck were the Roman fleets in Boulogne and Dover.

While barbarian pirates were contained by these defences, the south coast of Britain was safe. But Carausius's appointment coincided with a particularly intensive period of attacks, which might explain why Portchester was built. If the pirates had begun to penetrate the Straits of Dover regularly, bases for military operations would have been needed all along this ill-defended stretch of the coast. For this purpose Portchester could have been supported or superseded by the Roman fort at Pevensey, also set above a natural harbour about 80km (50 miles) to the east. This fort has recently been shown to be a work of the 290s and shares some striking architectural similarities with Portchester.

Recent excavations confirm that the fort was constructed between 285 and 290. First, there is a gap in finds of coins from the 290s, which suggests that the fort was deserted for a short period soon after it was completed. Second, there is little trace of buildings in the earliest phase of occupation, and such ditches and road surfaces as have been discovered look makeshift. It appears, therefore, as if the fort was constructed to deal with an immediate crisis but was then abandoned before being completed, most probably because Carausius's victories had rendered it redundant.

But Portchester did not remain vacant long: there is evidence that it was occupied once more from about AD 300, though how the site was developed is not clear. Indeed, the internal layout of the fort is poorly understood. Though archaeologists have uncovered a grid of roads, as well as rubbish and cess pits, they found little evidence for associated structures. It is probable that any evidence of timber buildings has been removed by ploughing and other subsequent development.

Finds of building materials hint at more substantial structures, possibly in areas that have not yet been excavated. Around the mid-fourth century new roads were built in the interior of the fort. These new roads might have been built as part of the improvement of the defences of Britain ordered by Emperor Constans (c.AD 323–50), who visited the province in 342.

Above: Roman items found at Portchester include, from top, an intaglio, an ivory fish counter, a cloak pin and a pot

Building the Roman Fort

Between the two D-shaped towers beyond the Landgate it is possible to get a good impression of the Roman defences. The walls still stand to what is probably their original height of 6.1m (20ft), although their upper levels and parapets are medieval. They were constructed in sections, and some of the vertical divisions between these are visible. The sections were raised in horizontal layers; a complete course of flints was set in position across the head of the wall and then covered with mortar, which bonded the stones together. Large flints were used on the faces of the wall, and double courses of large limestone slabs or red Roman tiles were used in some places to strengthen and level the masonry. Extensive refacing, both medieval and modern, has obscured these details in many areas. Wooden poles were also laid right through the original width of the wall to stabilize the structure while the mortar set. Some of the sockets for fixing the Roman scaffold are still visible in the masonry. This can best be seen from the interior of the fort.

In the Middle Ages, the inside face of the Roman wall around the outer bailey was quarried away as building material for the new castle and priory. As a result, the surface of the wall is very rough and slopes away at the bottom to a broad foundation. Only in the inner bailey does the wall preserve its original thickness. The fort is thought to have been enclosed on all sides by a double ditch.

Wooden poles were laid through the width of the wall to stabilize the structure while the mortar set

Above: The core of the Roman wall, which was built up with layers of flint and rubble
Below: A reconstruction drawing of Roman builders constructing the defences at Portchester, using layers of large limestone slabs to strengthen the masonry

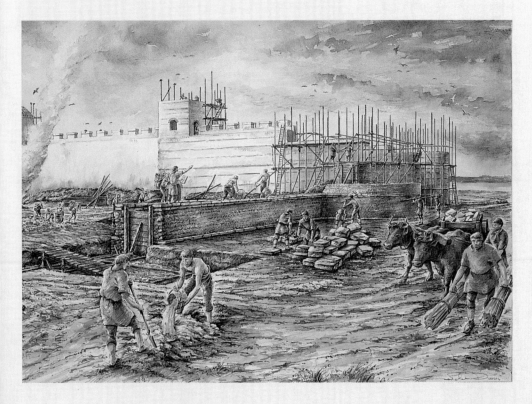

Manning the Fort

Among the officials listed in the *Notitia Dignitatum*, a list of the civil and military jobs in the Roman empire, is the 'Count of the Saxon Shore'

Right: The forts of the Saxon Shore, as illustrated in a medieval copy of the Notitia Dignitatum. *'Portus Adurni' on the bottom right may be Portchester*

Little is known about the community living at Portchester during the late Roman period. Burials of children within the walls from about 300 onwards suggest that a mixed community lived here at the time. It is possible that the population was entirely civilian and included soldiers only at times of crisis. Alternatively there might have been a permanent military presence either in the form of a garrison or of a community of 'laeti', paramilitary settlers drawn from other Roman provinces to secure the borders of the empire. There is very little evidence to indicate which is the most likely, and wider academic debates about the late Roman empire have been invoked to throw light on the problem. Crucial in these debates is a document called the *Notitia Dignitatum*, a list of civil and military posts in the Roman empire probably drawn up in the late fourth century. Among the officials it lists is the 'Count of the Saxon Shore', a commander of a series of forts along the south and east seaboards of England. Several of these forts can still be identified, but it is not clear if Portchester is among them. Nevertheless, some scholars have associated it with one of those listed, a certain 'Portus Adurni'.

Such an identification, if correct, would suggest that Portchester had an active military role in the fourth century. The term 'Saxon Shore' might be applied to these forts either because they served as frontier defences against pirates of Saxon origin or because the 'laeti' garrisoning them were Saxons. Whether or not Portchester is mentioned in the *Notitia Dignitatum*, some pottery and other finds from the excavations do suggest that the population of the fort had some Saxon connection.

SAXON PORTCHESTER

It is unlikely that the fort at Portchester was ever entirely
abandoned after the collapse of the Roman empire, but
evidence for its occupation during the fifth century is slight.
Pottery and other finds suggest the settlement of the site was
continuous from approximately 500 through to the Norman
Conquest of 1066. Owing to the limited evidence available,
it is difficult to say much about the physical appearance of
Portchester in this period, beyond the fact that the Roman
defences probably remained little changed. The density of
occupation within the fort enclosure evidently fluctuated, and
the development of the interior with buildings was irregular.
Some parts of the fort were ploughed and cultivated. Apart
from the foundations of several huts, the most important
structure to have been excavated is a tenth-century residence
with a hall and tower, possibly a belfry, in the south-west
quarter of the fort. Bell towers were one mark of the house
of a thegn – a man of knightly rank – so this might have been
a residence of some importance.

Documentary sources provide little further information
about the site in this period. An entry in the Anglo-Saxon
Chronicle for 501 records the death of a high-ranking man
during a raid on the area of Portsmouth, and it is possible that
he was killed at Portchester. But it is not until 904 that the
first unequivocal mention of Portchester occurs. In that year
Edward, king of the West Saxons, received Porceastra from
the bishop of Winchester. About this time the fort was turned
into a burgh, one in a series of fortified bases intended to
defend the kingdom of Wessex from Viking attack.

*Top: A Saxon coin of Burgred,
king of Mercia (r. 852–74), found
at Portchester*

***Above:** A Saxon spouted jug, found
at Portchester*

***Below:** A reconstruction drawing
of Portchester in the tenth century.
To the left of centre is the thegn's
residence, with its hall and tower*

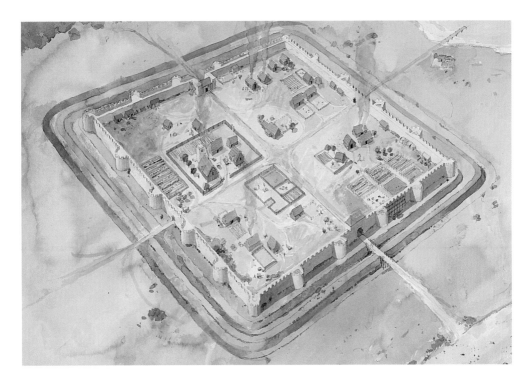

NORMAN PORTCHESTER

Right: Image from the Chronicle of England, showing Henry I and the White Ship disaster below, when Robert Maudit, owner of Portchester, was drowned together with Henry I's son in 1120
Below: The richly carved Romanesque font from the Augustinian priory church, which is now the parish church of St Mary

In the aftermath of the Norman Conquest of 1066, William the Conqueror (r.1066–87) granted Portchester to a powerful associate, William Maudit. Maudit probably founded the castle here, though when he did so is not clear. The Domesday survey of 1086 makes no mention of a castle, only a 'halla', or hall. But Domesday often fails to mention castles, and the defences of Portchester could already have been occupied. The form of Maudit's castle is also uncertain. He probably created the inner bailey, protecting its buildings with a ditch and timber palisade. He may also have built the 11th-century inner arch of the Watergate as part of a new entrance to the fort enclosure.

When William Maudit died in about 1100 his estates passed to his son Robert, another leading figure in Anglo-Norman politics. Robert was drowned with Henry I's son in the White Ship disaster of 1120 and the castle – still undocumented – is believed to have passed a few years later, on the marriage of Robert's daughter, to another powerful magnate, William Pont de l'Arche. He presumably held it until his death in 1148 and was probably responsible for redeveloping it in stone. Critical in dating and attributing his work, in the absence of documentary evidence, is the fabric of the present parish church of St Mary in the fort enclosure.

Before the end of 1128 William founded an Augustinian priory within the walls of the Roman fort. The foundation charter implies that a church already existed on the site, though no trace of this has yet been discovered. The present building, which now serves as the parish church, was constructed for his new community in the 1130s. A set of monastic buildings must also have been begun at this time, though nearly all trace of these has disappeared. Work on them may never have been completed, however, because between 1147 and 1150 the community moved to a new site at nearby Southwick. The architectural details of the church compare with the inner bailey wall and its associated buildings, including the keep, which may consequently be attributed to William. It is not clear who inherited the castle after the death of William Pont de l'Arche in 1148: either his son or a certain William Maudit, a descendant and namesake of the founder of the castle. Confusingly, the future Henry II (r.1154–89), while heir apparent to the throne, also granted the castle in 1153 to Henry Maudit, the son of William. This grant is the first document to record the castle's existence, but it appears not to have been honoured by Henry II when he came to the throne the following year. Instead he took over the castle as a great royal stronghold, in which role it continued throughout the high Middle Ages.

Left: A reconstruction drawing of Portchester in about 1140, following the construction of the keep and forebuilding. The low, squat proportions of the keep are typical of such buildings in this period

THE ROYAL CASTLE

Above: A 14th-century manuscript illustration of King John (r.1199–1216), who regularly stayed at Portchester to hunt in the neighbouring Forest of Bere
Below: A portrait of Henry II (r.1154-89) , who often visited Portchester, from the 13th-century Historia Anglorum

One consequence of royal ownership is that there is an increasing quantity of documentary information about Portchester from the 1160s onwards. Particularly valuable for the history of the early development of the castle are the so-called Pipe Rolls, the accounts of the royal exchequer. They record repairs in 1183 to a royal residence separate from the keep, which presumably stood in the inner bailey. The keep is also referred to in 1174, though the small sums then spent on it could not account for any major works to the building. It is generally supposed, therefore, that the 12th-century heightening of the keep took place before the castle came into royal ownership.

For Henry II, as for successive English kings, the importance of Portchester was due in large part to its situation commanding a harbour with easy access to the Continent. Visiting his vast territorial possessions stretching to the Pyrenees, Henry II regularly passed through Portchester, and it figured in his celebrated dispute with St Thomas Becket. Henry also used the castle as a prison for important captives such as the earl of Leicester and his wife, and as a safe haven for shipping his treasury to France in 1163. During the rebellion of 1174, the castle was made ready to withstand an assault. It was armed with catapults, the wall-walks were enclosed with wooden galleries called brattices and a garrison of 10 (later 20) knights was installed.

King John (r.1199–1216) visited the castle regularly during his reign and built a new chamber and 'wardrobe' here in 1211. With its neighbouring hunting park in the Forest of Bere it was an attractive site for royal recreation, and John is known to have brought his hounds here for hunting in 1214. The bones of birds used in the lordly sport of falconry have also been found in the late 12th-century levels of the excavations.

John's experiences of Portchester cannot have been entirely pleasant. It was probably here in 1204 that he heard the disastrous news of the fall of his own duchy of Normandy to Philip Augustus, king of France. And it was from Portchester that John launched two unsuccessful expeditions to recover his lost inheritance in 1205 and 1213.

In 1216 John's political misfortunes culminated with the invasion of England by Prince Louis, the son of Philip Augustus. Louis' invasion campaign was initially a triumphant success, and Portchester surrendered to him in June, after both London and Winchester had fallen. The castle was retaken in the spring of 1217 by John's successor, Henry III (r.1216–72). It was often used by Henry III as a point of embarkation and return for his campaigns in France.

During the reign of Edward I (r.1272–1307), the castle mill was repaired in 1289, and in 1296 there is record of a wooden tower being constructed to strengthen the Roman wall along the sea front. Fearful of French invasion, Edward II (r.1307–27) garrisoned the castle and between 1320 and 1326 set its

Left: A reconstruction drawing of the castle in about 1211. The keep was raised almost to its present height in the mid-12th century

Above: Edward III (r.1327–77) often stayed at Portchester and it was here that he prepared for his campaign that culminated in his great victory over the French at Crécy in 1346, shown here in this medieval manuscript illustration
Below: Henry V (r.1413–22) as Prince of Wales receives the Regement of Princes from its author Thomas Hoccleve, in about 1411. Henry V prepared at Portchester for his campaign against the French at Agincourt in 1415

buildings in order at a cost of over £1,100, then a very substantial sum. As part of this work he remodelled the buildings of the inner bailey and enclosed the keep forebuilding with new structures, now demolished. He also extended the main gate to the outer bailey and substantially reworked the Landgate and Watergate.

Curiously, within ten years, the castle and its defences were apparently again in serious disrepair. A survey of 1335 describes many of its buildings as ruinous and reports that the sea had broken through the south wall of the Roman fort. Edward III (r.1327–77) immediately undertook repairs, building a defence by the Watergate to prevent galleys from sailing through the breaches in the Roman wall. At the same time an outer defence was created along the landward side of the fort. After 1356 the domestic buildings of the inner bailey were extensively reordered, and in the following decade the sea wall was properly repaired. The castle was also garrisoned and fully armed. But the defences of Portchester were never put to the test. Nor did Edward III often stay at the castle, though in 1346 he prepared here for the campaign that culminated in his great victory over the French at Crécy.

The last important medieval alterations at Portchester were undertaken by Richard II (r.1377–99) between 1396 and 1399. Shortly after arranging a peace treaty with the French, he began work to the existing royal apartments in the inner bailey. At the same time the keep was remodelled and the Landgate recast in its present form. A complete set of building accounts survives for these operations, which were supervised by the master mason Walter Walton.

THE LATE MEDIEVAL AND TUDOR CASTLE

It is conventional to think of Portchester after the death of Richard II as passing into decline and obscurity, from which it was briefly reprieved by one notable event celebrated by William Shakespeare. In 1415, while Henry V (r.1413–22) prepared at Portchester for the campaign against the French at Agincourt, a plot to depose him was exposed. It was almost certainly within the castle walls that he confronted the conspirators – among them Richard, earl of Cambridge, Henry, Lord Scrope, and Sir Thomas Grey. Having found them guilty of treason, he had them sent to Southampton and executed.

But although Portchester was increasingly overshadowed in both economic and military terms by the developing town of Portsmouth, it was far from forgotten. Despite a depressing survey of 1441, in which the castle is described as being 'right ruinous and feeble', Portchester was chosen as the landing place for Henry VI's French bride, Margaret of Anjou, in 1445, and in the 1490s its buildings were repaired.

In October 1535, Henry VIII (r.1509–47) and Anne Boleyn visited Portchester Castle. In 1563 it was used as a military hospital for the sick and wounded from the French wars, and in 1583 its fortifications were put in readiness for a Spanish invasion. Elizabeth I (r.1558–1603) held court here in 1603, and shortly afterwards Sir Thomas Cornwallis, constable of the castle, completely remodelled the eastern ranges of the inner bailey. A survey of the castle made in 1609 by the royal surveyor, John Norden, describes the new buildings as 'containing four fair lodging chambers above and as many rooms for office below'.

Above: A portrait of Anne Boleyn, who visited Portchester in October 1535, with Henry VIII

Below: A sketch of the inner bailey, made as part of John Norden's survey of the castle in 1609. The drawing illustrates the full extent of the domestic buildings in the inner bailey

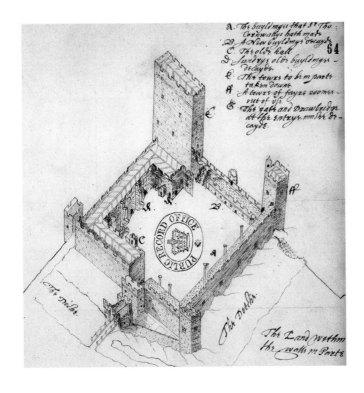

THE CASTLE AS A PRISON

In 1632 a local landowner, Sir William Uvedale, purchased the castle from Charles I (r.1625–49). Ownership of the castle has descended ever since through his heirs, the Thistlethwaite family. In 1644, during the Civil War, a detachment of Parliamentarian dragoons was briefly quartered here, but the castle saw no action. Twenty years later, in 1665, it was used to house about 500 prisoners taken during the Second Dutch War. Some of them were lodged in the parish church and were responsible for setting it on fire; the damage was not properly repaired until 1706.

The castle was pressed into service as a prison during all the major conflicts of the 18th century. Although it was first leased by the Crown for this purpose between 1702 and 1712, during the War of the Spanish Succession, the life of the prisoner-of-war camp is not documented in detail until Britain's various hostilities between 1740 and 1763. Complaints were made by the prisoners in 1742 about the cramped conditions, and there were riots the following year. In response, the Admiralty gave permission for a fenced airing ground to be constructed in the fort enclosure, the Roman walls being too ruinous to form an effective barrier to escape.

Overcrowding continued to be a problem, however, with the number of prisoners rising from 1,100 in 1746 to about 2,500 in late 1747 – almost a quarter of the prisoner-of-war population in England at the time. A system of exchanging prisoners with captured British servicemen meant that few remained in confinement for more than a year. The men slept on shared beds within a regulation space 0.75m (2ft 6in) wide and 1.8m (6ft) long and were fed a carefully prescribed diet provided by private contractors. Captured officers received pay of a shilling per day and were given considerable liberties, being allowed to leave the castle with a guard. In 1760 one French prisoner married a local woman, and a child of theirs was later baptized in the parish church. The prison guards themselves were poorly accommodated, with insufficient barrack space.

Above: A bone carving made by one of the prisoners at Portchester in about 1805

Below: A view of the interior of the castle, engraved in 1733, showing the prisoners milling around within a specially created exercise yard

An Inside View of PORTCHESTER CASTLE, in HAMPSHIRE. Dedicated to the Officers of the Militia.
Engraved from a Drawing taken on the Spot by an Officer

The Prisoners of War

Life within the prison during the Revolutionary and Napoleonic wars with France appears to have been regulated in much the same way as in the 1760s. But, reflecting the scope of the war, the prisoners came from across the globe. Besides Europeans and Americans there were also West Indians, who had to be issued with extra clothes to protect them from the cold. Foreign nationals were commonly recruited to the ranks of the British army, a situation that could spark trouble in the prison. In 1810, for example, 120 German and Swiss prisoners volunteered for the Sicilian Regiment, and when they went to collect their uniforms a riot ensued, the French threatening to kill them. Women, children and other civilians innocently caught up in the war were also held here, though they were usually exchanged with British prisoners or released as quickly as possible.

Prisoners came from across the globe. The West Indians had to be issued with extra clothes to protect them from the cold

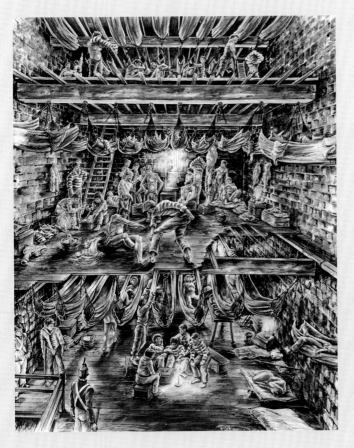

Above: Detail of some of the graffiti inscribed by French prisoners on the angle tower of the inner bailey
Left: A reconstruction of the interior of the keep, showing how it was racked out for the accommodation of prisoners in the Napoleonic wars. Conditions within the building must have been appalling

In 1760 Edward Gibbon, then a budding scholar of Roman history, briefly took command of Portchester as an officer in the Hampshire militia with '4 subalterns, 7 serjeants, 9 corporals and 214 privates to guard about 3,200 prisoners. The place was agreeable for the officers who boarded in neat private houses and lived very well, but it was very bad for the men. The prison was very loathsome and the men's barracks not much better.'

After the Treaty of Paris in 1763, Portchester was emptied of prisoners, and its medieval buildings, still under military control, were left to fall into ruin. But in 1794 work began again to fit it up for prisoners as Britain was stirred to war in the aftermath of the French Revolution. Thirteen new timber houses were erected in the fort enclosure to house 500 men each, and proposals were put forward to alter the keep and its adjacent buildings to hold 1,000 more men. The castle appears to have remained in largely this form for the remainder of its working life as a prisoner-of-war camp, which continued with an eight-year break between 1802 and 1810 (when it was used as an ordnance depot) until 1814.

Many of the prisoners practised crafts such as bone-carving, creating items such as combs, dominoes and devotional objects. The model ships made by them were particularly valued, and such was the quality of lace-making in the prison that it was forbidden as a threat to the local industry. Inmates could trade all these items along the main road of the fort, which was fenced off from the prison enclosure and accessible to the villagers. In 1811 some prisoners were caught forging money.

For entertainment a theatre troupe was organized, and its productions included *The Barber of Seville*, sung to

Above: A portrait of Edward Gibbon, the Roman historian, who briefly took command of Portchester as an officer in the Hampshire militia in 1760

Below: A view of Portchester in about 1770 showing Ashton's Tower and the keep beyond. A sentry stands guard beside the Roman postern gate

Miners at the Castle

Edgar Long was born in September 1915, during the First World War. His father had a baker's shop at 200 Castle Street, opposite the Cormorant pub. Edgar's first memory of Portchester was walking along Castle Street on Armistice Day 1918 and watching the procession with all the children waving flags.

'When I was a child, I used to play around the castle and swim in the sea there. I remember that some of the boys used to dive off the castle walls at high tide. I also remember the walkway being built around the seaward side of the castle during the Depression in the 1920s.

'They brought Welsh miners here and a lot of unemployed people and they used them to dig out the inner moats of the castle. They built a sea wall from Hospital Lane right round the castle and they filled in behind that with all the excavation material that they dug out. It took a couple of years and they had a little railway running down from inside the castle. It was pushed by hand and then pulled back by a horse. They used little trucks – like miners' trucks.'

'I remember the Welsh miners digging out the inner moats of the castle in the 1920s'

Top left: Miners at work by the Landgate in the 1920s
Above: Edgar Long and his friends playing near the castle in 1924. Edgar is second from the right
Left: Miners' trucks were used to take the soil away

Above: A view of the castle as a prison by a former prisoner, dated 1817. It illustrates the degree to which the interior of the fort was built up

Below: Portchester today showing the external east face of the fortress wall

the accompaniment of a 12-piece orchestra. The last prisoners of war left the castle by May 1814, after which it served briefly as a hospital and then as a prison for deserters. In 1819 it was finally abandoned by the army and returned to the Thistlethwaite family. They presumably demolished most of the remaining prison buildings. A proposal was made in 1855 to convert the castle into a military hospital, but a purpose-built one was constructed instead at Netley, near Southampton. The castle stood as a ruin for more than half a century until, in 1926 the Thistlethwaites placed it in the guardianship of the Office of Works, which undertook a massive clearance operation. Many of the workers employed in the project were unemployed miners. In 1984 the castle passed into the possession of English Heritage, in whose hands it remains.